10-MINUTE
BIBLE STORIES

To my wonderful grandchildren
~ Naomi, Samuel, and James

10 MINUTE

BIBLE STORIES

Anna Adeney

LION
CHILDREN'S

Published by
Lion Hudson Limited
Wilkinson House, Jordan Hill Business Park
Banbury Road, Oxford OX2 8DR, England
www.lionhudson.com

ISBN 978 0 7459 7887 1
e-ISBN 978 0 7459 7888 8

First edition 2021

Acknowledgments
Illustrations by Gareth Williams

A catalogue record for this book is available from the British Library
Printed and bound in the UK, February 2021, LH26

Contents

Contents

Escape from Egypt

I moved my heavy mortar and pestle nearer the open doorway so I could hear what was happening next door. I had to hurry as I was making fresh toothpaste for Lady Wia. I'd already ground up the mint, rock salt, and black pepper, so I quickly sprinkled dried iris flowers onto the mixture and ground hard.

I was lucky as most of my friends and their parents slaved in the hot sun, making bricks from mud, sand, and straw. Almost all of us Israelites were outdoor slaves, here in Egypt, making bricks and then making buildings and roads with them. But my mother was Lady Wia's bath slave and I was able to help her instead. She and her husband were really rich, as Ramose was a very important scribe. He worked for Pharaoh Ramesses himself.

Most people bathe every day in the River Nile, which is close by. But rich Egyptians took baths indoors, with slaves to serve them. We filled, emptied, and cleaned the bathtub, heated the water on the fire and poured it over them, then applied their cleansers. I had learned how to make soap, deodorant, and toothpaste, but mostly I did the hard, boring things like emptying and cleaning the bath. That didn't stop me listening in though! Lady Wia was fond of my mother and told her all sorts of stories while she was relaxing in her bath. There were amazing things happening in Egypt.

I'm called Tamar and my mother's name is Miriam. She was named after her grandmother, who is Moses' sister. Moses is the leader of the Israelites who have been in Egypt for more than four hundred years now. Well, not me, of course, because I am only ten! But Moses wanted to lead the tribe out of slavery in Egypt to the land that God had promised us.

Grandmother Miriam is incredible! She's really old, older even than Moses and his brother Aaron and they are ancient! But she's so bright and interesting and still sings and dances like a young girl. She taught me that God had promised our ancestor Abraham three things.

First, that he would have many descendants – that's us, the Israelites. There were so many of us that the Egyptians were frightened, even though we were still slaves. Second, that there would always be a special relationship between us and God. The Egyptians could never have that because they had *hundreds* of gods to worship rather than the one true God. Third, God promised us a special land of our own to live in. That's what Moses was striving to get for us, just as God commanded him, but Pharaoh would not let us go!

Sometimes Pharaoh said he would let us go, but he always changed his mind. Moses kept trying. He had been up against Pharaoh's magicians and was beating them at every turn. Egypt had been struck by so many bad things – plagues they call them, each one worse than the last. It began with the river water turning red! Then there were hordes of locusts, thousands of frogs in the houses, millions of gnats and flies, skin diseases, and more! *That's* what Lady Wia goes on about in the bathtub! She was worried about the rumours that the next plague was going to be really bad. *I* was praying that it would make Pharaoh let us go at last.

Both of us were right. The day passed slowly, until sunset when we were allowed to go to our own homes. Moses was spreading the word to all the Israelites. Each family had to roast a lamb and put some of its blood around our doors. We ate the lamb with bitter herbs to remind us of our suffering in Egypt. We had to get ready to leave at any moment, with our cloaks on, and the bread dough stuffed into bowls and pots and wrapped in our blankets. No yeast though, to make the bread rise. It wouldn't be ready until morning and we were leaving right away. We had to eat flat bread from then on.

We left to the overwhelming cries and wails of the Egyptians, as they realized that the firstborn of every human and animal was dead. Because of the blood mark above our doors, all of the Israelites had been spared this plague. Before I knew it, we were on the road.

We could only take what we could carry

or load onto our animals. Because I was
part of Moses' family we were at the front,
ahead of the thousands of other Israelites.
When the land got higher I could look
back and see the line of men, women,
children, sheep, and goats. It seemed to go
on forever. The Israelites were walking out
of slavery!

I was so excited at first, but it was
hot and dusty and Moses hardly ever let
us stop and rest. He was worried that
Pharaoh, who'd told the Israelites to leave
Egypt, would change his mind and come
after us. Everyone followed Moses, but
many people complained and argued.

"Why don't we go through the land
of the Philistines?" asked one. "It's the
shortest way."

"They are our enemies," answered
Moses. "If we become part of a war the
people will want to run back to Egypt!
We'll take the road through the desert,
toward the Red Sea."

The most amazing thing about this dirty, exhausting journey was that God was with us. He led us the whole time! During the daylight He became a curling pillar of cloud, so high I couldn't see the top of it. Even people right at the back of the line could still see the cloud. As soon as it got dark, God changed into a bright pillar of flames that led our way. When the pillars stopped, we knew we had to stop and camp. God spoke to Moses all the way, ensuring he made the right decisions for the Israelites.

We took tents on our journey to shelter us from the cold at night. Each big tent held an extended family. I was in the same tent as my mother, Grandmother Miriam and her brothers, Aaron and Moses. There were other members of the family too, but I slept close to my mother and great-grandmother.

I know all about God talking to Moses, because he, Aaron, and Grandmother

Miriam would talk about it every night. They thought I was fast asleep, but I found the sudden journey scary and often found it hard to get to sleep. Although God mostly spoke to my great-uncle in private, Moses discussed it all with the family elders and I couldn't help hearing everything. Maybe they're so old that they're all going deaf because they talk really loudly, even when they're trying to whisper!

One day, God said to Moses, "Tell the Israelites to turn around and camp between Migdol and the sea. Camp on the shore of the sea opposite Baal Zephon. Then Pharaoh will think that you are lost. He'll realize how hard it will be for Egypt now all his slaves are gone. He'll come after you with his army and I will use them to show the Egyptians that I am God."

This journey took us through areas of salt marshes and lagoons, windy places where papyrus grows. Then the pillar stopped beside the sea and we settled down to rest. We'd been camping there some days when we heard panicked voices.

"The Egyptians are coming!"

"There are hundreds of horse-drawn chariots and armed soldiers!"

"Why did you make us come, Moses?"

"We were better off as slaves in Egypt than dead in the desert!"

But God knew what He was doing and He told Moses exactly what to do: "Speak again to the Israelites. Order them to get moving. Hold your staff high and stretch your hand out over the sea. Split the sea! The Israelites will walk through the sea on dry ground. Meanwhile I'll make sure the Egyptians keep up their stubborn chase. I'll use Pharaoh and his entire army to put My glory on display so that the Egyptians will realize that I am God."

It sounded impossible. How can anyone walk through the sea? But Moses obeyed God and spoke to the people.

"Don't be afraid. Stand firm and watch

God do His work of salvation for you today. Take a good look at the Egyptians as you're never going to see them again! God will fight the battle for you. Obey me and keep quiet! God says we must move on."

Then, before our amazed eyes, the pillar of cloud moved from ahead of us to behind us, so it was between us and the advancing Egyptian army. Ahead of us was a sea full of reeds, the strong east wind rippling the water and the papyrus fronds.

Moses lifted his arms and the east wind roared as loud as a pack of lions, whipping up the water to expose the seabed! He set out, striding into what had been the sea, only minutes before. I was really scared! But Grandmother Miriam grabbed one of my hands and my mother the other. We followed Moses into the sea. Everyone followed, marching across the seabed as quickly as we could.

It took ages for all the Israelites to cross. The first groups lingered on the far side, worried whether everyone would make it across. There was a terrified silence as the last of the flocks and their shepherds crossed the seabed. We could see the Egyptian chariots clearly now, gaining ground.

Then there was a murmur as the heavy chariots seemed to bog down in the muddy ground we had so recently sped across. But the army of fierce soldiers who followed them were still terrifying! However, the Egyptian army was having second thoughts. Voices floated toward us.

"Run from Israel!"

"God is fighting on their side and against Egypt!"

God told Moses to stretch out his hand over the sea again. I followed him to the shore and watched as he raised his arms once more. Then I looked out to see how close the terrifying army was getting. But I saw nothing but waves rippling across the salty sea. Everyone saw the miracle that

God had done and knelt in reverent awe before Him. The Israelites put their full trust in Moses to lead them to the Promised Land.

What a celebration we had then! Grandmother Miriam grabbed my hands and danced wildly with me. Everyone joined in, dancing and singing, "I will sing to the Lord, for He has triumphed gloriously!"

The Incredible
Talking Donkey

I wandered down toward the marketplace,
knowing some of the other boys would
be gathered by the well, refreshing
themselves with fresh water. There were
lots of people around, but they all tended
to gather in groups, depending on what
sort of jobs they did.

The donkey boys were there, as usual,
comparing notes on their busy day.

Although quite young, we all had a job, working hard, either for our families or for a master. My master is called Balaam and my name is Josh. I'm the youngest of the donkey boys so I usually just listen in to all their boasting and arguing.

"My father's bought a new donkey!" said Seth excitedly. "It's the most beautiful donkey in Pethor."

"Donkeys aren't beautiful!" said Levi. "Who cares for beautiful anyway? My master's best donkey is the fastest donkey in Pethor – probably in the entire world!"

"But my donkey can carry more than both your donkeys put together!" said Zedekiah scornfully. "That's what donkeys are for, after all. What can be better than that? My donkey is surely the best of all."

At last I had something to say to these older boys, but would they even listen?

"That's nothing," I said quietly. "My master's donkey can talk!"

The boys all turned and looked at me,

as if they could hardly believe I'd dared to open my mouth. There was silence for a moment and then they all started to laugh.

"Donkeys can't talk!"

"Do you expect us to believe that?"

"That donkey must have kicked you in the head, Josh, if you believe stuff like that!"

"Come on then, camel-head," jeered Zedekiah. "What makes you think your master's donkey can talk?"

"I heard it!" I said. "It talked to my master quite distinctly. And I saw an angel on the road to Moab! A real angel, with a sword and everything! I could tell you all about it, but I don't think my master would like that."

The boys looked at each other and laughed again. But they were intrigued, just the same. I could see that they didn't believe a word of it, but everyone likes a good story.

"Go on, Josh, tell us about it!" said Levi.

"We won't say a word to anyone, will we boys?"

I got nervous then. My master would be angry if he thought I'd told people. But everyone talked about their master's doings, didn't they? And nobody *ever* listened to me. I was really tempted.

"If I tell you about it, you must promise not to tell *anybody*," I said.

The boys promised.

"It all started with the Israelites," I said.

"I heard the men in the marketplace talking about them," said Zedekiah. "Haven't they got a huge army camped beyond the Jordan, at Jericho?"

"That's right," I said. "King Balak of Moab was sure they were going to invade his country and overrun it because the Israelite army was so much bigger than his. So he sent for my master, Balaam."

"Balaam's not a warrior!" said Seth. "What good would he be in a battle?"

"Don't you know that Balaam's a

famous soothsayer?" I said.

"That's right!" said Levi. "I've heard that when Balaam curses somebody, they stay cursed! Really bad things happen to them when he says the word."

"I've heard that too," admitted Zedekiah. "God listens to Balaam. I'd hate to get on the wrong side of him. Tell us what happened, Josh."

"I fetch and carry and wash the dishes in Balaam's house, as well as looking after the donkeys," I said. "So I'm always about the house and I get to hear everything that goes on. It all started when King Balak sent messengers to Balaam. King Balak wanted Balaam to curse the Israelites, so they'd die.

"They brought lots of money for him. Balaam loves money so he asked them to stay over and he'd give them an answer in the morning. Then he went up onto the roof to ask God what he should do. I had to go up with him in case he suddenly needed anything.

"'Don't go with these men from Moab,' said God to Balaam. 'I don't want you to curse the Israelites, because they are my blessed people.'

"Balaam was obviously disappointed, but he did what God said.

"'God won't let me go with you,' he told King Balak's men, 'so you'd better all go back home.'

"Next time King Balak sent out even more important people to Balaam. They brought lots more money this time too. Balaam looked at the money and sighed.

"'Even if King Balak offered to fill my house to the rooftop with gold and silver, I can't come unless God says I may... Josh, make up beds for my guests!' he called. 'Tonight I'll see if God has changed His mind.'

"That night he talked to God again.

"'Don't you think I should go with them, Lord,' asked Balaam, 'just to find out what all this is about?'

"'Go with them then,' said God. 'But you must say exactly what I tell you to say.'

"'Money, lovely money,' I heard Balaam gloating to himself as I followed him downstairs.

"'Saddle my best donkey for me, Josh,' he said, very early next morning. 'We're going to Moab!'

"The Moabites rode on ahead, followed by Balaam, with me behind on our smallest donkey. We were riding along, when suddenly my master's donkey stopped. Balaam nearly went head first over the donkey's ears! He couldn't see what the terrified donkey saw and yelled loudly with annoyance.

"I could see – and so could the donkey – that it was an angel holding a sword. The donkey was very frightened and turned off into a field.

"'Get back on the road you stupid beast!' yelled Balaam.

"As he hit the donkey and pulled her

back onto the path, the angel moved further down the road.

"The poor donkey tried to squirm past the angel by pressing against the wall. This squashed Balaam hard against the rough stones.

"'My foot! You're crushing my foot, you good-for-nothing ass!' he roared. He beat her hard with his stick until she walked on.

"Then we came to a narrow place where the donkey couldn't pass the angel, so she lay down in the road. Balaam was furious and beat her even harder.

"Suddenly God made the donkey talk, just like a person.

"'Why have you beaten me three times?'

"'Because you're making a fool of me!' roared Balaam furiously. 'If I had my sword I would kill you!'

"'Do I usually behave like this?' asked the donkey.

"'Well... no,' admitted Balaam.

"Then God must have opened Balaam's

eyes to what the donkey had seen all along. Balaam saw the angel standing in the road with his drawn sword, and Balaam fell on his face.

"'Why have you beaten your donkey three times?' asked the angel. 'If she hadn't got you out of my way I would have killed you with my sword and saved her life.'

"'I'm so sorry! Please forgive me!' moaned Balaam. 'I was greedy for money, that's why I wanted to go to Moab. Shall I go home now?'

"'No, go to meet King Balak,' said the angel, 'but say only what God tells you.'

"We continued on to Moab. When we reached the Arnon River, King Balak was there to meet Balaam.

"'Why didn't you come right away, Balaam?' asked King Balak. 'I only want to thank you and give you lots of money and power.'

"'Well, I'm here now,' said Balaam crossly. 'But don't depend on me to do just what you want me to. I can only say what God tells me to say.'

"King Balak sacrificed many fine oxen and sheep, and Balaam and the princes of Moab dined well that night. I just carried the food – and maybe nibbled a leftover or two.

"Next day King Balak wanted results.

"'Get your men to build me seven altars,' said Balaam. 'Then bring me seven bulls and seven rams.'

"They did so and Balaam sacrificed the animals and then went to talk to God, who told him exactly what to say.

"'You brought me here to curse the Israelites,' said Balaam. 'But how can I wish bad things on them when God does not want this to happen? He wants only good things for His chosen people.'

"'What are you saying?' asked King Balak angrily. 'I brought you here to curse them and you want to bless them?'

"'I can only say what God wants for

them,' said Balaam calmly.

"'Come with me to another place,' said King Balak. 'I'm sure when you see the Israelites from there that you will want to curse them!'

"So we went on and seven more altars were built. A bull and a ram were sacrificed on each.

"The king waited impatiently for Balaam to return from talking to God.

"'What did your God say this time?' he demanded.

"'God is not a man, King Balak,' said Balaam. 'He doesn't tell lies and He doesn't change His mind. He brought the people of Israel out of Egypt and He loves them! I cannot curse them. I can only bless them.'

"'If you aren't going to curse them, at least don't bless them,' said King Balak furiously. 'We'll go to Mount Peor. Maybe your God will let you curse them from there.'

"Balaam and I knew for certain now

that God wanted the Israelites blessed, not cursed, but King Balak made the seven sacrifices again anyway.

"Balaam looked out across the desert toward the camp of the Israelites, which stretched across the plains.

"'God has told me that He will bless the Israelites and give them the Promised Land,' he said. 'Israel will be a mighty race and defeat all their enemies. Anyone who blesses Israel will be blessed himself. But anyone who curses them will be cursed himself!'

"King Balak was livid with rage.

"'I could have made you rich, but your God has kept you from that! Get out of here! I never want to see you again!'

"'I told you that I can only say whatever God wants me to, no matter how much gold and silver you offer me,' said Balaam sadly. 'I warn you, King Balak, that Moab will soon be defeated, as will the other tribes nearby... Get the donkeys saddled,

Josh. We're going home!'"

"That's incredible!" said Zedekiah.

The other boys murmured agreement.

"Did you ever hear the donkey talk again?" asked Seth.

"Never!" I had to admit. "Even though I brush her and pet her every day. I bring her extra fresh hay and ask her how she's doing. But she doesn't even say, 'Thank you!'"

David and Goliath

"That sheep with the bent horn seems to have disappeared again!" I yelled to my friend Jethro. "Have you seen her?"

He shook his head and we both continued searching. There was nothing but rocks and scrubby little trees – and other sheep, of course. But not the lost ewe with the bent horn. Then Jethro, standing on a high rock nearby, yelled and pointed downhill with his shepherd's crook. I raced down and found the sheep, lying on her back with her legs in the air.

"Not again!" I groaned. I'm tall for my age, and strong, but still not yet the size of my grown-up brothers – and the sheep was heavy! I buried both hands in her grubby fleece, leaned back, and *heaved*. It took four tries to get her rolled onto her feet once more and I got several hard kicks for my trouble. I watched Bent-Horn stagger off to join the rest of the flock and breathed a sigh of relief. Sheep suffocate and die very quickly once they get stuck on their backs.

My father, Jesse, has a farm in Bethlehem but I, as the youngest son, have to tend the sheep on the hills above the town. He would be angry if I'd lost one of the sheep and my seven big brothers would make so much fun of me!

"Look, David!" yelled Jethro. "Someone's coming!"

A man was running up the slope toward

us. I recognized Obed, one of our family servants.

Great! I hoped he was coming to say that King Saul had commanded me to come and play the harp for him again because he was depressed.

I liked the king and prayed for his good health, and the food King Saul sometimes shared with me was much tastier than what I eat as a shepherd boy. Jethro and I were always hungry, so I'd much rather be with the king than here.

"Your father says to come down to the farm at daybreak and take some food to your brothers at the battlefield," said Obed, "but you must make sure all the sheep stay safe."

Our tribe, the Israelites, was at war with another strong local tribe, the Philistines, and my three eldest brothers were part of the army.

"How's the battle going?" I asked. "It's been forty days now. Surely our army has defeated those wicked Philistines by now!"

"Nothing's happened yet," said Obed gloomily. "The Philistines have picked a champion – a *giant*, so I've heard! 'Goliath' they call him. Every day he comes out and curses our army. He challenges one of *our* lot to come out and fight him – just one. Then, if he defeats our man, *all* of the Israelites will be slaves of the Philistines."

"But if *our* man wins, won't that make all the Philistines slaves of King Saul?"

"Exactly!" said Obed. "But nobody's got the courage to challenge him. They're all terrified!"

"That can't be true!" I shouted angrily. "My brothers are there. Hasn't even *one* of them challenged this Goliath?"

"They're all too scared," repeated Obed, "and now I'd better get back to the farm."

So I was up at dawn, running down toward the farm. I'd promised Jethro I'd bring him back a good meal if he looked after the sheep alone for a few days. My father, Jesse, was waiting for me.

"Take this food, a sack of cracked wheat and these ten loaves of bread down to your brothers in the battle camp in the Oak Valley. These ten wedges of cheese you must take to the captain of their division. Then come back quickly and bring me news of how your brothers are doing and how the war with the Philistines goes."

So off I went. As I neared the battlefield I could see that the Philistines were on one big hill, with the Israelite army on the opposite hill, and a valley between them. I headed for the Israelite camp, to find my brothers. Just as I arrived I saw both armies move into position, facing each other, battle-ready. It took a while to find my brothers among all the other warriors. While we were talking together, the Philistine champion, Goliath of Gath, stepped out from the front lines of the Philistines, ready to roar his challenge.

I could hardly believe my eyes. The giant looked ten feet tall! His bronze helmet looked big enough for Bent-Horn to take a bath in! Goliath was dressed in metal so strong I'm sure no sword or spear could pierce it. He wore bronze shin guards and carried a bronze sword. Even Goliath's spear was bigger than me!

"That spear tip alone is very heavy," whispered my brother Shammah, as if the giant might be able to hear him, "and what they say his metal coat weighs is a lot more than *you* weigh, little brother!"

"I hear *you* are too scared to go fight him, big brother!" I said hotly. "It's so embarrassing! Is *every* Israelite here a coward too?"

I soon got my answer, as Goliath began his challenge.

"It's been forty days now," roared Goliath. "I'm calling on you, Saul's men, for the last time. Don't bother using your whole army! Am I not Philistine enough for you? So pick your best fighter and pit him against me. If he gets the upper hand and kills me, the Philistines will all become your slaves. But if I kill him, you'll all become our slaves and serve us. I challenge the troops of Israel today. Give me a man. Let us fight it out together!"

But nobody came forward from the Israelite army.

"That Philistine is destroying the integrity of Israel!" I yelled. "Who does he think he is, taunting the armies of a God who is alive and powerful? Someone must stop him! What does King Saul say?"

"The man who kills the giant will be famous," they said. "The king will give him a huge reward, offer his daughter as a bride, and look after his entire family."

Eliab, my oldest brother, heard me talking with the men and lost his temper.

"What are you still doing here, David? Why aren't you minding your own

business, tending our sheep? I know what
you're up to. You're nosing down here
just to avoid working!"

"What's the matter with you?" I said.
"All I did was ask a question!"

Some men ran to the king, to tell him
what I was saying. I was relieved to hear
that King Saul wanted to talk to me and
immediately ran up to his tent.

"Master, don't give up hope," I said,
bowing to the king, "*I'm* ready to go fight
this Philistine."

"You can't go and fight Goliath!"
said King Saul. "You're too young and
inexperienced! He's been a warrior since
before you were born."

"Don't forget, my king, I've been
tending sheep for my father since I was a
little boy. Whenever a lion or bear came
and took a lamb from the flock, I'd go after
it, kill it, and rescue the lamb. I would
kill any predator. And I'll do the same
to this Philistine pig who is taunting the

troops of our God. God will give me *His* power against this unbeliever! God, who delivered me from the teeth of the lion and the claws of the bear, will deliver me from this Philistine!"

"Go then," said King Saul, "and may God help you!"

"But not like that!" said the king, as I turned to leave. "At least put on my armour, to help keep you safe!"

Then Saul helped me put on his own soldier's tunic. His bronze helmet went on my head and he belted his sword on over the tunic. I could hardly move. The helmet was too big and everything weighed a ton.

"I can't even *walk* with all this stuff on me. I'm a shepherd boy, and those are the skills I will use."

I took it all off and went out dressed in my usual tunic. Going down to the brook I selected five smooth stones. I put them in the bag hung around my waist. Then, with my sling ready in my hand, I walked back to the battleground. With God, I knew I could *do* this!

As Goliath paced back and forth, he suddenly noticed me, standing with my shepherd's staff in my hand. He took one look at me and sneered.

"You are a little boy, a mere youngster, not even old enough to grow a beard! Am I a dog that you come after me with a stick? Come on, I'll turn you into a tasty morsel for the buzzards and ravens."

Then he cursed me by the gods of the Philistines.

I may not have been grown up yet, but I wasn't a little boy. Even if I was, that wouldn't matter, because God was on *my* side. So I stood my ground.

"You come at me with sword and spear and battle-axe," I yelled. "I come to you in the name of God-of-the-Angel-Armies, the God of Israel's troops, whom you curse and mock. Today God is handing you over to *me*. I'm going to kill you, cut off your head, and serve up your body and the bodies of your Philistine buddies to the vultures and wolves. The whole world will know that there's an amazing God in Israel. *Everyone* here will learn that God doesn't save by means of sword or spear. The battle belongs to *God*. He has already won this war!"

That enraged Goliath and he started running toward me, brandishing his huge spear. The whole Israelite army gasped at the sight. I ran toward the Philistine. Then, suddenly I stopped, reached into my pack for a stone and put it into my slingshot. Goliath was still thundering violently toward me. I took a deep breath and hurled the stone. It hit the giant so hard that it sank deeply into his forehead. It felt as if the whole earth shook as the Philistine crashed, face down and dead, into the dirt.

Then I ran up to Goliath and stood over him, pulled the giant's sword from its sheath and cut off his head. When the Philistines saw that their great champion was dead, they scattered, running for their lives.

How the army of Israel cheered as I held up the Philistine's head! Then they charged after the Philistines. After killing or capturing many, the Israelites came back and looted their camp. I suddenly realized that, even though I was only the youngest son, I was never going back to being a shepherd boy.

The Fiery Furnace

My sandals pounded the steep path as I sprinted home, desperate to tell my sister all I had seen today. My father sent me home earlier than usual, so Lilith would still be busy with her household chores. Abba (my father) obviously had not wanted me to see the execution – as if I was a little boy and not a ten-year-old worker! But I had hidden and seen it all. Lil would *not*

believe it. I hardly believed it myself and I'd
seen it with my own eyes!

A figure raced down the hill toward
me, dodging through the groups of people
and donkeys, setting dogs barking and
women muttering disapproval. A young
girl shouldn't be running like that on a
public street unless her house was on fire!
Lil must have been laying out washing to
dry on the flat roof of our house, seen me
coming, and come to meet me.

Everyone knew about the incredible
statue of King Nebuchadnezzar that men
had been building for months now. But
it had been hidden from view on the
open plain, behind wooden scaffolding
and thick leather sheets – and guarded by
soldiers. It had been unveiled only a few
days ago and the whole city was buzzing
with awe and amazement. The royal
household and local lords had already
been to bow before the statue, amid music
and great partying. Now the merchants

and guilds of craftsmen were taking their turn. I was proud that my father had the biggest brick kiln in all of Babylon. I was now a worker and able to see the incredible statue close up long before the ordinary people. Lil was *so* jealous. But at least if she heard about it from me she could tell all her friends before *they* were able to go and bow down before it.

We nearly collided on the path, but Lil grabbed me by the wrist and hauled me down a nearby alley.

"Tell me!" Lil commanded breathlessly. "Tell me all about the statue!"

"Never mind the *statue!* Something much more exciting and important happened after we saw it. It was incredible! We didn't make any bricks today at all. We had to fill the kiln with..."

"Forget the stupid bricks, Shad!" said my sister crossly. "That's all you talk about, every day. Bricks, bricks, bricks! I'm sick of it. Tell me about the king's statue. Now!"

I sighed. My sister was two years older and had recently grown quite a bit bigger than me. The unbelievable miracle would have to wait its turn.

"I went with Abba and all the brick workers to see the statue. Soldiers were there and took all our names and directed us where to go. We walked a long way to the plain – and then I saw it. The sun reflected from it so fiercely it hurt my eyes. I just stood there, amazed, till Abba yelled at me to shut my mouth and stop gawking. He shoved me so hard in the back that I fell down on my face and got a mouthful of dust! All around me, the other bricklayers were lying with their foreheads pressed to the ground."

"But what did it look like? Is it true that it's as big as the mountain and covered with real gold?"

"It certainly looked like a tower of gold," I said, even though I had never seen a bit of gold in my life. "It shone like the sun itself.

It wasn't as big as a mountain though. I asked Abba on the way back and he said it was as big as eighteen or twenty men, all standing on each other's shoulders. You know how good Abba is at estimating measurements for buildings made with our bricks."

"Forget the bricks!" said Lil. "Did it have his clothes – and a face like the king?"

"Up close it nearly blinded me with its brightness. We weren't allowed to stay to look much, the soldiers just wanted us to bow down. But I walked backward beside Abba when we left. Then I could see the carving that decorated the statue. That showed the clothes and his face. Then the tanners came to take our place. They didn't half stink! I had to hold my nose as we went past. Did you know, Lil, they soak their leather in old pee to soften it?"

"I don't want to know! Tell me more about the golden statue!"

"You'll see it for yourself soon enough!

Can I tell you about the miracle now?"

"Miracle, what miracle? You saw a miracle and you're babbling on about bricks and smelly things! What were you thinking?"

I sighed again. Sisters! I would never understand them.

"Abba hurried us all back to work," I said. "He wasn't best pleased because we hadn't finished filling the kiln with wood. Then we worked hard all day, putting more and more and more wood in the kiln..."

"This better not be about bricks," warned Lil.

"We didn't bake any bricks today. That's what I'm trying to tell you. The king had ordered Abba to fill the kiln with lots of wood because he wanted to bake men! Or maybe that should be to roast men," I said doubtfully.

"They can't do that, you silly little boy! Bake or roast, it would kill them!"

"Exactly! It was meant to be an execution."

Lil's eyes went as big as cowpats.

"Tell me," she whispered.

"We filled the big kiln with wood, five to *seven* times as much as we'd use for baking the bricks. Then Abba told me I could go home, that I'd worked hard enough for one day. *That* was weird for a start. I wanted to see the fire lit – it would have been huge! But Abba made sure I left. So I started to come home and tell you about the statue, as I'd promised. But there was a commotion on the road – a group of men and soldiers coming from the palace. People were saying that the king himself was coming to Abba's brickyard! So I doubled back behind the soldiers, climbed that little hill behind the brickyard, and hid in the bushes."

"Was it the king?" asked Lil.

"It certainly was! There were lots of soldiers guarding three men. You would have liked seeing *them*, Lil. They wore beautiful, fine robes and jewels – and they were young and looked just like princes!"

"Were they the ones they were going to... roast? But – *why*?"

"I know that too," I said, glad to know something that my big sister didn't. "I heard the king talk to them. They were from Judah and the king had captured them with all the other Jews. I'm sure it was years ago, when they were about our age. Now they all had important jobs at the palace and the king really liked them."

"Why did he want to kill them then?" asked Lil.

"It was because of the king's statue. You know everyone was ordered to bow down to it? Well these men refused to bow down. They said that, because they were Jews, they would only bow down before the Lord, their God. I know their names too. One – the best-looking one – was called Shadrach, *like me*! The others were Meshach, and Abednego."

"So what happened next?" asked Lil.

"Well, the king was so angry! By then the whole kiln was well alight and it looked like a fiery furnace in there. The soldiers pulled the men over to the open door. 'This is your last chance,' said the king. 'Will you go to my statue and bow down and worship me?' The soldiers looked hot and sizzling being that close to the blaze, but the young men didn't even look a bit frightened."

"What did they say?"

"They told him that they would never bow down to the golden statue, or any Babylonian gods, even if they were killed because of it! Then they said that *their* God was able to save them, even from a fiery furnace! They were so sure of themselves, Lil, even with that raging fire burning at their backs. I'll never forget their words."

"Only the mightiest God *ever* could save them from being burnt to death," said Lil, in wonder at the mere thought. "Surely there is no god more powerful than fire?"

"That's obviously what the king thought," I said. "He told the soldiers to tie them up with rope so they couldn't escape. Then he told them to throw the Jews right into the middle of the fire. So that's what the guards did. They used their long spears to push them right into the heart of the fire!"

Lil gasped, but said nothing. She could hardly believe what I was saying. But then, I could hardly believe it myself, and I'd been there!

"I couldn't even watch at first," I admitted. "I just rolled behind the bush and waited for it to be over. Then I heard the king and the courtiers all making such a ruckus, screaming and shouting! Then everything went silent. It seemed that even the birds stopped singing and the dogs stopped barking. Then I peeped out. I could see the open door of the furnace, right below me. You're not going to believe this, Lil, but I saw four men walking around inside that fiery pit! They looked as if they were all just off home for their supper, not walking around inside a roaring furnace! There were those three young men from the palace – and another person too. He was all white and shining somehow. Oh, I can't explain it, but I've never seen anything like it!"

"Maybe he was an angel," whispered Lil, her face shining with wonder.

"At last the king called out to them. 'Shadrach, Meshach, and Abednego, you who serve the Most High God, come out of the fire, and come to me.' And they did. The shining man had vanished and just the three young men came out. They looked cool and spotless. Their ropes had all burnt off them, but their clothes weren't even singed. They didn't even look *dirty*, Lil, they didn't even smell of smoke. They still looked like rich young princes. Their amazing God had saved them! That's when

King Nebuchadnezzar became convinced that the Jews' God was the one true God and blessed Him."

"How do you know that?" asked Lil.

"He immediately made a law that nobody in Babylon could say anything against their God. If they did, that man would be cut in pieces."

"So it looks as if we *all* have a new, really powerful God, here in Babylon," said Lil. "Race you home, Shad? Last one there is a brick!"

Daniel in the Lions' Den

I put the wine jar down beside King Darius.
As usual, nobody took any notice. Two of
the three government leaders were with
the king and they did *not* look happy. I
picked up the empty jars and crept quietly
back to the kitchen.

My name is Amata and I work in King
Darius's palace. My mother, Ishtar, the
chief cook, was busy stirring a pot.

"Carry this vegetable stew down to Daniel's room, Amata – but no tasting on the way!"

My mother was smiling. She knew Daniel was a kind and humble man and would probably offer me a taste himself, even though I'm only a servant girl and he's another important government leader.

"King Darius said how well Daniel was doing as a leader," I told her. "You should have seen Bull's face! It looked like a ripe plum. I thought he was going to burst with anger! And Mule looked like he'd swallowed a cup of vinegar!"

The government leaders were not really called Bull and Mule. They had long, Persian names that I can't remember, so I gave them nicknames to suit their looks and characters. Luckily, such important men never went into the kitchen, otherwise I would surely be tossed into the lion pit.

"Didn't the king notice their reaction?" asked my mother.

"He didn't seem to," I said.

"He thinks so highly of Daniel that he can't see that the others are really jealous."

We live in Babylon, which was conquered years ago by the armies of the Medes and Persians. Darius was sent to be king and had divided the large country into one hundred and twenty regions, each with their own ruler. In charge were these three leaders. But Daniel was not originally from Media or Persia. When he was a young boy he lived in Judah, but he was captured by the Babylonians. He was clever and well-educated and had risen to one of the highest positions in the kingdom. King Darius loved him as a best friend and depended on Daniel for everything.

"Keep your eyes and ears open, Amata," my mother said. "Those two would love to get Daniel into trouble. If you hear anything, you can warn him."

But Daniel was such a good man that we weren't really worried. He'd lived in Babylon for more than fifty years now and served three different kings. Everyone had always respected Daniel. Bull and Mule hated Daniel because he was cleverer and more popular than them. They were petrified that King Darius would promote Daniel to be the highest minister in the land and then they'd have to take orders from him.

I loved listening to their conversations, so I could tell my mother all the news, as she hardly ever got a chance to leave the kitchen. I flitted around the palace constantly, so small and unimportant that I was almost invisible.

It was the very next day and hardly an hour since Bull and Mule's last meal.

"Girl, bring us wine and roast lamb. Now!" roared Bull.

"Don't forget the grapes, dates, and figs," yelled Mule.

They were a greedy pair and kept

me busy running back and forth to the kitchen. But that meant I could hear their plans.

"We have to do *something*," muttered Mule. "Or that wrenched Jew will have both our jobs!"

"He's probably aiming to be king himself! What can we do?" bellowed Bull.

"Shhh! Word must never get to King Darius that we're out to get Daniel," said Mule.

"Let's just have him killed! You can kill anyone if you have enough power and money – and we have both!"

"That's too dangerous," replied Mule quickly. "Darius would surely find Daniel's killer. We can't risk any whispers getting back to the king."

"Daniel must *die*!" hissed Bull.

Horrified, I shivered behind the pillar. What were they going to do to Daniel?

"Yes, of course he must die," agreed Mule. "But I have the most cunning idea.

If we arrange this right, then no blame can ever fall on us. The king loves Daniel, the people love him – even the slaves love him! Daniel does nothing bad, nothing against our laws – *nothing* we can get him for."

"He prays to that God of his constantly," said Bull, "surely that ought to be against our laws."

"Exactly!" said Mule. "Darius is our king, but he is also a man. I'm sure he wants to hear that he is the greatest king ever – the best Babylon ever had. We will tell him so and..."

"What good would that do?" shrieked Bull. "We want him to realize that *WE* are the greatest – not him and *especially* not Daniel!"

"*Quiet*," whispered Mule. "Nobody must know. We'll encourage King Darius to celebrate how wonderful *he* is, and persuade him to make a law that nobody in Babylon must worship or pray to anybody but himself for a whole month. Anybody that does so will be thrown to the lions! By the time Darius realizes that this will involve Daniel, it will be too late. Daniel will be dead!"

Behind the pillar, I felt really scared. Even I knew that Babylon was ruled by the laws of the Medes and Persians. That meant that once a law was made, even King Darius could not change it. Daniel could not escape the lions.

I tiptoed out of the room, then ran as fast as I could toward Daniel's room. I was so worried, I burst in without knocking. Daniel was standing at his open window, praying to his God. He always does this, three times a day. I knew better than to try to talk to him now. I crouched down outside his door and waited.

When his prayers were over Daniel opened the door and let me in. Seeing I was upset, he sat me down, and poured me a drink, as if I was the master and he was *my* servant.

"What's the problem?" he asked kindly. "Can I do anything to help?"

I blurted out everything – how Bull and Mule hated Daniel and their plan to have him not only killed, but eaten!

"You must go to the king right away and tell him," I begged, "before it's too late!"

"It's already too late," said Daniel. "Besides, I trust in my God. God will protect me."

"But it's the *lions*, Daniel! Great, huge, hungry lions! In the kitchens the lion keeper said that he'd been ordered not to feed them. Mule's been planning this for ages! Can't you stop praying to your God for a month? Or just do it quietly, behind closed doors?"

"Nothing will ever stop me praying to God," said Daniel. "Nor will I try to hide it. But don't worry, Amata. All will be well."

At dinner, instead of their usual complaints and criticisms, Bull and Mule flattered and praised the king endlessly.

He'd obviously been so surprised at the
change in them that he'd agreed to the new
law without even taking time to think about
it. For several days Bull and Mule watched
Daniel closely and reported back to the
king. I shook with fear as I watched them.

"Remember the law you made, King
Darius, that nobody could worship or pray
to anyone but you? Daniel continues to
open his windows three times a day and
pray loudly to his God. He has deliberately
broken your law. You must throw him to
the lions!"

King Darius was horrified. How could
this have happened? He knew that Daniel
was the best of men – and his friend. He
spent the rest of the day trying desperately
to think of a way to get around the law. But,
when Bull and Mule came back, he had
nothing. The law of Medes and Persians
must rule.

"Daniel has broken the law," he agreed,
reluctantly. "He must be thrown to the

lions. Now leave me. I will not forget your part in this!"

Bull and Mule were too excited to worry about this warning. They rushed to arrest Daniel. I ran to the kitchen to tell my mother that Daniel was about to die. Soon everyone in Babylon knew about it.

Daniel walked nobly to the lions' den, still strong and looking fit and healthy, even though he was now an old man. In the crush of officials and soldiers, nobody noticed me.

The keepers rolled back the stone above the pit. The angry roars of hungry lions bounced from the stone walls. Light flooding through the gap showed three huge, ravenous lions.

King Darius looked at his friend Daniel.

"May your God, whom you serve continually, rescue you!"

Then the king returned to his palace, full of sorrow and guilt.

"Toss Daniel into the pit!" thundered Bull.

The lions roared even louder as soldiers threw Daniel through the hole. Then the keepers rolled back the big stone door and everyone sighed with relief.

King Darius refused to eat any of the good food I brought to him. Nor would he be distracted by his entertainers. He spent a sleepless night, alone and heartbroken.

As soon as the sun rose, King Darius ran from the palace to the lions' den, his officials and servants – and me – hurrying after him.

As soon as the stone was removed, the king called out.

"Daniel, servant of the living God, has He been able to rescue you from the lions?"

"May the king live forever!" Daniel shouted back.

At the sound of his voice everyone surged to look into the pit.

The lions were lying close to Daniel, keeping him warm like a trio of enormous shaggy dogs.

"My God sent His angel and he shut the mouths of the lions. They have not hurt me, because I was found innocent in His sight. Nor have I ever done any wrong to you, your majesty."

King Darius was overjoyed. They threw down ropes and Daniel was pulled up. He did not have a single wound, not even a scratch, from the hungry lions, because he had trusted in his God.

Bull and Mule had already run away, but the king soon had them captured and dragged back to the lions' den. The ravenous lions got their meal at last.

Then the king made a new law.

"Everyone in my kingdom must worship the God of Daniel, for He is a living God who will stand forever. He rescues and saves. He performs signs and wonders in the heavens and on this earth. He has rescued Daniel from the lions!"

So Daniel continued to flourish and to serve the king and the country.

And what a story I had to tell in the kitchen!

Through the Roof!

My name is Judith and I'm nine years old.
I live with my parents who I call Abba
(Father) and Eema (Mother), and my uncle.
Uncle is paralyzed and cannot walk. We all
praise and thank God every day that Abba
has such a good job, building houses in
our prosperous town of Capernaum. This
means that Uncle does not have to sit by
the crossroads and beg just to keep alive.
Instead he lives with us and his friends
often come in to visit him.

I was outside, watching for Abba. Then I saw him in the distance. I was just about to jump down and run in to tell Eema to put the fish on to cook, when a group of men joined him and he stopped to talk. *Abba!* I thought. *Hurry up, I'm starving!*

I went inside, got Uncle's food and laid it down beside him. Then Abba burst through the door.

"Jesus has come back to Capernaum!" said Abba in great excitement. "He's come back from His journey. They say He's healed a leper and many others! He really *can* work miracles, just as we thought. We must go and see Him immediately!"

"Let's eat first," said Eema, and she put the food on the table.

Although anxious to see and hear Jesus, Abba's day had been long and hard, so he gave thanks for our food and we sat down to eat.

"We are taking my brother to Him," said Abba. "I'm sure Jesus will heal him, if

we just ask Him. He could make him walk
again!"

Make him *walk* again! Surely that was
impossible? Uncle had been ill so long that
his legs were as thin as sticks and strangely
twisted.

"How could this man, Jesus, make Uncle
walk again?" I asked.

"They say that He's not just a man,"
said Abba, "although He does call Himself,
'The Son of Man'. We think that He is the
Messiah, sent by God to save our people.
If He can work miracles, then He *must* be!
Who can work miracles but God?"

All of us looked at Uncle. He had
stopped eating and gone very pale.

"Do you really think that would be
possible?" he asked. "I dream about it
sometimes, you know – walking again."

He fell silent then, but I could imagine
what he might be thinking. That he could
go out whenever he wanted, and not
have to wait until there were four strong

men free to carry him outside the door. That he could climb the hillside outside Capernaum and see the wild flowers and the lambs playing in the spring. That he could wade out into Lake Galilee and feel the water surging around his legs. That he could work like a man once again. I felt tears rolling down my cheeks. Could Jesus really do that for him?

Just then, the three men who build houses with Abba arrived at the house.

"We need to leave now!" said the biggest of Abba's friends. "Jesus isn't resting, as they told us. Nobody would let Him! He's teaching in Peter's house. Half of Capernaum is there already. We need to go, right away, or there will be no room for us."

Abba and his friends immediately went over to Uncle's mattress and each took a corner of it.

"Lie down or you'll fall off!" said Abba. "Don't be scared. Jesus really can heal you. We just have to ask Him."

Uncle was trembling with fear, so I took his hand and walked alongside them. I thought they might say I couldn't come with them because I was just a little girl and this was men's business. But he knows how Uncle depends on me, so Abba let me come. They practically ran through the streets, carrying the mattress. I could hardly keep up and poor Uncle rolled about and nearly fell off several times!

When we came to the house we couldn't even get near the door. There were so many people that they'd spilled out into the street, crowding the doorway, many men deep.

"Make way!" Abba cried out in his strong voice. "Let my poor paralyzed brother through. He needs to see Jesus!"

But nobody would let us through. It was a solid wall of people all pushing to try to get closer to the Teacher and straining to catch His words of wisdom. Uncle was in danger of being knocked off his bed by the people coming after us. Abba led the way back to safety. They put Uncle down on the ground and rested a bit, all lost in thought.

"Maybe I'm not meant to be healed," said Uncle hesitantly. "Maybe I'm not good enough. Let's go home again – before I get trampled underfoot!"

"I've got an idea," said Abba. "We are all builders. We know exactly how these houses are made and what they are made of. We'll take the outside staircase up to the roof. Then we'll dig our way *through* the roof until we've made a hole bigger than the mattress. Then we'll lower him down to Jesus. The Teacher can't fail to see him then. And He'll heal my brother. I know He will!"

Abba's friends obviously thought that this was a brilliant idea and each grabbed a corner of the mattress again. Dig through a *roof!* My mouth fell open in surprise. Uncle started trembling again. I was lost for words but clung tightly to his hand as we headed back to Peter's house. Thankfully, the outside staircase to the roof was on the side of the house and, with a lot of pushing and shoving, we got there.

The men steered Uncle and his mattress up the staircase. They laid him down on the roof and Abba and his good friends breathed a sigh of relief. I'd hoped we'd be able to hear from up there and maybe attract Jesus' attention – somehow. I couldn't imagine how anyone could dig a hole in a roof! But Abba and his friends all took out their big knives from their belts and started to thrust them into the hard mud of the roof. Uncle looked terrified.

"Wait!" Uncle begged. "This is impossible! How can you lower me down to Jesus? The roof is higher than His head. Your arms aren't as long as a man's height. I will still be such a long way from the floor. Are you just going to drop me onto Jesus' feet? My legs are ruined already! You'll break my arms and my head and my neck too! Please don't do this to me!"

But Abba and his friends were determined. They believed in Jesus and His healing power.

"Trust in Jesus," said Abba. "He will not let you down – and neither will we. Judith, run back home and bring me the coil of rope that is hanging on our back wall. Run! As fast as you can."

So I ran. Thankfully we lived not far away. I grabbed the rope and ran back to Peter's house with it, struggling up the staircase once more. Already the men had pried away the top layer of hard mud. Abba had told me that roofs were made by laying tree branches across the top of the stone walls. Then small branches, reeds and palm fronds were laid on top of that. Next came leaves, dirt, and finally the mud clay, which was rolled flat with stone rollers.

The men had already got through to the leafy filling and now I could hear lots of angry voices from below. I imagined all the muddy bits and leaves falling onto people's heads and had to stop myself from giggling. Abba cut the rope into four long pieces and the men were tying them to each corner of the thin straw mattress. Then they attacked the roof with their knives again until a small hole appeared. Using their great strength, the men pushed the long tree branches together so the hole became bigger and bigger.

Although I was scared, I couldn't help but lean forward and peer down through the hole in the floor. I'll never forget that sight! People were packed into the room like olives stuffed into a jar of oil. Everyone was looking up at us. Their faces looked a bit like olives too, all their mouths open wide with astonishment. There were lots of people whose faces I recognized, as well as many, many strangers. Men, women, and children, even a bunch of Pharisees huddled up together so they didn't touch any of the common people.

Pharisees are the *very* religious people,

who follow all the rules to the letter and stop to pray dozens of times a day, even if they are in the middle of the street. I'd heard Abba say that the Pharisees were very critical of Jesus, always trying to get Him into trouble. I guess that's why they were there.

After that first moment of shocked silence, everyone started yelling at once. They were brushing their clothes off and sneezing from the dirt and dry leaves showering down on them. Abba gently pushed me aside and the four men started lowering my poor uncle through the hole.

There was my uncle, his bed lowered right in front of the man who must be Jesus. He was shaking with fear. Jesus put His hand out toward Uncle.

"Don't be afraid, my friend," He said.

Abba called down from the roof. "Please heal my brother, Jesus. He's paralyzed. We know You can heal him! We believe in You!"

Jesus turned back to Uncle and said, "Your sins are forgiven."

These words really upset those Pharisees. They looked outraged and angry.

"He can't say things like that!"

"It's blasphemous!"

"Only God can heal sins!"

Jesus looked at the Pharisees and said, "Which of these things do you think is easier to do? Saying to a paralyzed man, 'I forgive your sins,' or saying, 'Get up, take your bed with you, and walk away?'"

Everyone looked both astonished and confused at these words. Then Jesus spoke again and pointed at Uncle.

"But, so that you all know that the Son of Man has authority on earth to forgive sins, I say to you, get up, pick up your bed, and go home."

Before our astonished eyes, my uncle stood up, bent over to roll up his mattress, stuck it under his arm, and made for the door, praising God! The people parted to let him out, rubbing their eyes in amazement. Then they praised God too!

Even I could see that Jesus had true power and that His power could only come from God.

From the rooftop, Abba called down to thank Jesus, then we all ran home to celebrate with my new strong uncle. I was so happy that Jesus had seen the faith of my father and his friends and had healed Uncle.

Next day all five of them went back and mended Peter's roof!

Feeding the
Five Thousand

I ran up the stony street from the shore
to my house, clutching two slippery fish.
I was pleased that my father had given me
quite big ones, as I'd be sharing them with
my two big brothers, who always ate like
ravenous wolves!

When I reached home my mother was
just laying out the freshly baked loaves to
cool.

"Can you put in an extra loaf for me, Eema?" I asked my mother, as she put together the meal for my brothers.

"Four loaves is more than enough," she replied. "Your brothers will share with you, Jared. And you'll be home for supper, after all."

"Pleeeeease, Eema," I begged. "They'll take two loaves and a fish each and I'll be lucky if I get to suck the fish scraps from the bones! *And* I have to climb that big hill to get to where the goats are. I'll be *starving*!"

"I suppose Gad and Eli *are* big eaters," she said. "It's their age. Don't worry, Jared, you'll catch up – eventually!"

Eema laughed kindly and added another thin round loaf of bread to the goatskin bag.

People, especially my big brothers, are always teasing me because I'm still quite small. I'm seven, and the youngest in my family of five brothers and one sister. Abigail is ten and helps Eema at home.

There's a lot to do. Just grinding the grain to make flour for the daily bread can take up to three hours! I help her sometimes because she gets blisters on her hands from all that grinding. Gad is thirteen and Eli is fourteen and they look after our goats on the hillside beside the lake. Abel and Zeb are even older and help my father, Asa, in his fishing business.

I'm looking forward to being a fisherman when I grow up. I love being out on the water, despite the high winds that often make the big lake feel really dangerous. But I'll have to look after the goats for years first, even though I won't be starting until I'm eight.

"Eema, have you heard about that amazing teacher, Jesus?" I asked, suddenly remembering what all the fishermen had been excitedly talking about down by the shore. "Titus just sailed back from Cana and he said that Jesus had healed a sick boy, without even seeing him!"

"Really?" asked Eema. "Whose boy? And how could Jesus do it?"

"I think they said it was an official from the king's court. His son was dying. He heard that Jesus had come back to Galilee, so he journeyed a long way to ask Jesus to come back with him and heal his son. The man *begged* Him, Titus said. He really believed that Jesus could heal his boy."

Eema shook her head as if she didn't believe it, but Abigail was eager to hear the rest of the story.

"So what happened?" she asked impatiently.

"Jesus told him, 'You can go home now. Your son lives,'" I said.

"The man believed what Jesus said and headed home. On his way back, his servants met him and shouted, 'Your son's alive!' The man asked them what time he began to get better. They said, 'It was yesterday afternoon at one o'clock when he suddenly recovered.' The father knew

that that was the very moment Jesus had
said, 'Your son lives.' That's what Titus said
anyway. Everybody's talking about it!"

"That's incredible!" said Abigail. "A real
miracle!"

"But did Titus actually see it for
himself?" asked Eema.

"No," I said, "but everyone's..."

"...talking about it!" interrupted Abigail
with a giggle.

"They can talk all they like," said Eema.
"But I won't believe in these so-called
'miracles' until I see one with my own eyes
– or somebody I know and trust sees one!"

I set off on the windy path up the hillside
with my mother's words echoing in my ears
and my brothers' dinner in the goatskin bag
bouncing on my back. I'd love to see Jesus
and listen to Him talk. Everyone said that He
told such good stories – and I love stories. I
think the best is the one about the shepherd
boy, David, killing the giant, Goliath. The
story of Daniel and the lions is good too.

Even better than a good story would be to see Jesus perform a real miracle! Every day in the marketplace I heard people whispering about the amazing things that Jesus did. But making a boy like me better when he was dying was hard to believe. I really wanted to believe in Jesus, but what if it was all just stories?

I hadn't got very far up the hillside when I heard a murmur behind me. I turned and saw a small group of men, also climbing up the hillside. I'd come to a wide, flat bit of the hill, so I stopped to have a little rest. I'm not nosy, really, but I was curious to see what was happening. Usually all you see this far up the hill is sheep and goats who have wandered from their flocks – and maybe a shepherd boy like Gad or Eli crossly chasing them.

The men sat down for a rest too. One of them was clearly the leader. He was much calmer than the others, who all looked stressed and anxious. The murmur turned into a loud babble, as if a huge festival was taking place nearby. Around the rocky outcrop I'd just passed appeared more people. And more and more and more! There must have been hundreds of them, maybe even thousands! I'd never seen so many people all in one place, let alone on this lonely hillside.

Seeing the first group of men sitting there, all the followers stopped and looked toward them, as if expecting something important to happen. So many people were there that I didn't feel bad about creeping closer, until I was right beside the first group of men.

"This is awful!" said one of them crossly. "Jesus needs to rest and to eat. Why won't they just leave Him alone for a few hours?"

"Don't worry," said the calm man. "They only want to listen – and learn. We must help them."

So that calm man was Jesus! I was seeing Him for myself for the first time.

His eyes were shining and He looked gentle and kind. Even if He was tired and hungry He didn't look cross. Suddenly I remembered what I had in my bag. I tugged on the cloak of the nearest man. The man he was talking to called him Andrew. He looked kinder than the cross man.

"I've got some food Jesus can have," I said. "I've got four – no, five loaves and two fish in my bag."

I took them out and showed them to Andrew.

Jesus called out, "Philip, where can we buy bread to feed these people? They've been following us for hours. They must be hungry."

Philip answered, "Two hundred silver pieces wouldn't be enough to buy bread for each person to get a piece. We don't have the money to feed anybody!"

Andrew took me by the arm and led me up to Jesus.

"Look, Jesus," he said. "There's a little boy here who has five small barley loaves and two fish. He's willing to share his meal with You – but that's not enough for a crowd like this."

Jesus looked at me with a smile that I will remember forever. Then He turned to His followers.

"Make the people sit down."

The grass was green and fresh here, not yet nibbled away by goats and sheep. The people sat down.

"There must be about five thousand people here," said Philip. "How can we feed them all?"

Then Jesus took the bread and gave thanks to God for the food. He gave it to the people who were seated in the front. Then He did the same with the fish. The people passed the bread and the fish around and everyone ate as much as they wanted. Still there was food left!

When the people had eaten their fill,

Jesus said to His disciples, "Gather the leftovers so nothing is wasted."

Some of the people had empty baskets with them. Maybe they'd been going to buy fish from fishermen like my father when they'd joined the crowd following Jesus. The men went to work and filled twelve large baskets with leftovers from my five barley loaves and two fish. I could not believe it!

The people were amazed too. Everywhere people were exclaiming and shouting out to each other.

"God is at work here!"

"He fed us all with just that little boy's lunch!"

"That's a miracle!"

"Another miracle! Jesus has performed another miracle!"

"Jesus is truly the Prophet! God's Prophet right here in Galilee!"

"God must be telling us that Jesus should be King here!"

"Yes, we must make Jesus our King!"

They all turned and started to come forward as if they were going to make Jesus a king, whether He wanted to be one or not! But Jesus had already disappeared and hidden himself farther up the mountain. There are lots of caves and hidden places up there, so I guessed Jesus was safe from the crowd. I breathed a sigh of relief.

I'd better be getting up the hillside myself. My brothers would be famished by now. They wouldn't share so much as a crumb! But that didn't matter to me, because I'd had enough food to last me for a long time. Then suddenly I realized – I'd given away my brothers' food! I had nothing to take to them. They'd certainly be amazed at the story of the miracle I'd seen Jesus perform. Unfortunately they'd never give me the chance to tell the story!

Just then Andrew walked past me, carrying one of the big baskets of leftovers.

He smiled at me and that made me brave enough to explain my dilemma.

"I was taking that food to my big brothers," I said. "They're tending our goats farther up the hillside. They'll be really hungry by now. They'll be really angry too!"

"Jesus doesn't want anything wasted," said Andrew.

He took my bag and stuffed it full of bread and fish. My brothers would listen to my story about Jesus after all. I ran up the hill and yelled to them with excitement.

Even more importantly, that evening I would tell Eema the story of how Jesus really did feed five thousand people with the food she'd packed for my brothers. She would know for sure that Jesus could and did work miracles. My mother would believe me!

Raising a Dead Girl

Tali and I were talking and giggling together when her mother came home from the early morning market with a huge basket of fish. My name's Rebecca and I'm eleven years old. I've lived next door to Tali my whole life and we are best friends and do everything together. Only the boys go to school, of course, but we learn all the skills we need to know from our mothers. Today I was going to help out at Tali's house.

"Talitha, can you and Rebecca take all these fish up to the top floor and lay them out to dry in the sun?"

Tali and I both wrinkled our noses and exchanged a fed-up glance – smelly fish were *not* one of our favourite things – but we knew better than to complain.

"No need to make those faces!" laughed her mother. "I asked the fisherman to gut them for me down by the shore, so all you need to do is to flatten them out and lay them on the racks to dry. Here, I'll put them into two baskets for you to take up. Then, when you're done, I've got some fresh dates and figs for you."

That cheered us up a bit. Fresh figs and dates from the market would probably be plump and luscious, much tastier than the dried ones we usually ate. When the fish were divided up I grabbed the biggest of the baskets and started up the stone steps to the open room on the top floor. Tali is tiny, much smaller than me, even though she's a whole year older. That's why everyone calls her Talitha, which means "little girl". So she struggled even with the weight of the smaller basket. Tali and her family have a bigger house than mine as her father, Jairus, is the leader of the synagogue in Galilee, the area where we all live.

Up on the flat roof it was cooler and the fish didn't smell as bad in the open air as they had downstairs. I started laying out the fish close together on the racks before Tali even made it up the stairs. I wondered why she was being so slow. Putting out the fish to dry was not the worst of our usual chores, after all. Having to cut them open and pull out their guts was much worse! We often had to do that too. Eventually she made it upstairs and started to lay out the fish in her basket.

I chattered away to my friend, continuing our earlier conversation, hardly noticing how quiet Tali had become.

I was looking forward to the festival coming up and Tali's father had promised her a new scarf. We'd been discussing which design she should choose. Then I turned around to help her finish off her basket. Tali was curled up in the corner, her arms clutching her middle, and her face a very strange pale complexion.

"Tali, what's the matter? Is it the smell of the fish? Have you got a pain?"

Tali just gave a little moan. I hurtled down the steps to get her mother.

"Talitha is sick! I don't know what to do!" I wailed.

"Tell her to come down and get a drink and some fruit. That will make her feel better," said her mother calmly. "I'll get some water from the well."

I ran upstairs again but I couldn't get Tali to move. Her mother came up with a bowl of water and cloth. She tried to get Tali to drink but she just couldn't do it. She wet the cloth and wiped Tali's face with it.

"Can you lay out Talitha's sleeping mat next door please, Rebecca?"

On hot nights families slept on the top floor, where the roofless area kept them cooler than the dark lower floor. I ran and grabbed the bedding and laid it out. Then I helped her mother carry her over to her bed. Poor Tali couldn't walk. She couldn't even talk! For hours we watched over her. Tali's mother looked really worried.

Neighbours came in and out suggesting different things, but nothing made her any better. Suddenly somebody said, "Can't you see that the little girl is dying? You'd better fetch her father from the synagogue before it's too late!"

Tali *couldn't* die. She was too young! But everyone around me was convinced of it. The three men who worked Jairus's land would soon be home for their meal but Tali's mother didn't want to wait that long to send a message to Jairus.

"Rebecca, run to the synagogue and tell

Jairus that Talitha is very sick! He needs to see her before she dies!"

I had been crying for ages but this at least gave me something useful to do to help my friend. I rushed down the stairs and through the narrow alleyways until I arrived at the synagogue. I yelled at the first person I saw to fetch Jairus.

When he came out I grabbed his arm and told him what had happened. Then I tried to pull him in the direction of home.

"Talitha's been really sick *all day*! Everyone says she's going to die! You must come straight home!" I cried.

Instead of heading back toward the house Jairus turned toward the lakeside. I grabbed his sleeve.

"Come home! They say Talitha is *dying*!"

"We must find Jesus, the Healer," said Jairus. "He's just come back from Gerasa. You won't believe the things I've heard, the people He's healed! I must find Jesus. He's our only hope!"

Jairus turned away and went off in search of this man, Jesus. I wanted to get Jairus back home as soon as possible, so I followed him closely, clutching the side of his cloak. The nearer we got to Jesus, the harder it was. Crowds of people pressed close to the Healer. I had never seen so many people. But Jairus pushed through the crowds until he was right next to Him.

When he saw Jesus, he fell to his knees and begged, "My little daughter is at death's door. Come and lay hands on her so she will get well and live."

"I will come with you," said Jesus.

Amazingly, the whole crowd tagged along too, pushing and jostling, trying to stay close to Him. They wanted to see another miracle too. I stayed close Jairus's side, determined not to be left behind or pushed over. Glancing over my shoulder at the throng of people, I kept getting glimpses of a woman behind us. She was stretching out her hand, as if she was trying to touch Jesus, but the crowd kept jostling her away. The poor woman looked so sick and tears poured down her thin cheeks. I felt very sorry for her, but nothing could stop the rushing crowd. Then there was a bit of a scuffle behind us as people tried to get nearer to Jesus and I couldn't see her anymore.

Suddenly Jesus stopped dead in the street.

"Who touched Me?" He asked.

His followers all looked amazed and said, "What are You talking about? With this crowd pushing and jostling You, You're asking, 'Who touched Me?' Dozens of people have touched You!"

"I know that somebody touched Me," said Jesus. "I felt My power going out to someone. Who was it?"

There was a loud murmur from the crowd, then they parted to show that same poor woman who had been behind us. But she looked so different! The tears were gone and her face looked bright and shining.

"It was me!" she said, coming to kneel at the feet of Jesus. "I have had a terrible disease for twelve years and it's been so horrible and so painful. No doctor could cure me – although they all took my money! I have heard so much about You, Jesus, and I really believe in You! I knew if I could just touch Your clothes that I would be healed. But there were so many people around You. Then, when I got close, someone shoved me and I fell – but my hand just brushed the hem of Your robe. That was all I wanted to do. I knew Your power would heal me! Now I am well again. Thank You, Jesus!"

Jesus said to her, "Daughter, your faith has made you well. Now you're healed and whole. Go in peace and live a blessed life!"

As Jesus was comforting the woman, Jairus's workers came up and spoke to him.

"Come on home now," they said "You

don't need to bother the famous Teacher anymore. Talitha has already died."

When Jesus heard this He said quietly, "Don't worry about that, Jairus. Just keep trusting in Me and everything will be fine."

I cried again when I heard Tali had died, but something in this man, Jesus, made me believe in Him too, so I didn't give up hope – and neither did Jairus. We all headed back to the house.

"What's all this gossip about?" Jesus said to all the friends who were waiting in Tali's house. "Go back home, all of you. The child isn't dead. She's just sleeping."

Everyone began to complain.

"That's nonsense!"

"She's dead alright, I was there when she passed!"

"Who does this guy think He is, telling us such nonsense!"

"Peter, James, and John, you can come in with Jairus and Me," said Jesus. "The rest of you, be on your way."

The crowd grumbled as the men went inside, but they did as Jesus said.

I crept up the stairs behind them all, past the racks of drying fish and into the sleeping area. Tali's mother knelt by her bed, crying, and my best friend lay there, still. Jesus went over and took her hand.

"Get up, little girl," He said.

Talitha immediately sat up and smiled at everybody, then got up and came over to me. Everyone laughed and shouted with joy while Tali looked confused and a bit embarrassed that everyone had been watching her sleeping in the middle of the day.

"The child needs something to eat," said Jesus, with a smile.

"Oooh, yes, fresh figs and dates!" said Talitha. "Come on, Rebecca!"

She grabbed my hand and pulled me down the stairs toward our promised snack. As we went down I heard Jesus say to her parents, "Don't say anything about this to anyone."

That was the day I'll never forget, when
I saw this amazing man, Jesus, heal not one
but *two* people!

Miracle at Gethsemane

"This is a very interesting time to live in Jerusalem."

That's what my father said. I wouldn't say it was interesting, I would say it was amazing! So many incredible things have happened in the last three years and they all revolve around one man, Jesus of Nazareth, a carpenter's son. But that's not what His followers say. They say that He is the Son of God Himself.

Of course, I haven't known about Him for three years as I was only ten when

He started and not really interested in politics and religion then. But, since I turned thirteen, my father has been teaching me many things, so I can take over his job when I am older. My father, whose name is Malchus, is a very important servant in the house of Caiaphas, who is the high priest, the leader of the Temple in Jerusalem. He is the head of the Jewish supreme court, which is called the Sanhedrin.

Malchus is my name too, but I usually just get called Mal. We come from a proud Arab tribe of the nearby Nabatean desert. When my grandfather was a young boy, old King Herod waged war on Nabatea and won, which is how my family were brought to Jerusalem. Now my father is a really important person in the household of Caiaphas.

My father is really clever and Caiaphas depends on him to represent him in important meetings. Recently the high priest, and everyone about him, has been getting really upset about what Jesus is doing. Although Caiaphas is the head man for the Jews, the Romans rule all of our land and everyone is scared of them.

The important Jews hate Jesus because the people respect Him more than them. They also hate the way Jesus loves the common people and is always with them. He doesn't follow all their silly rules either and will even heal people on a holy day. Caiaphas is worried that Jesus' success in attracting followers will lead Rome to punishing everyone in the whole country. The Romans hate it when people don't follow all the rules. And Jesus doesn't!

Let me tell you what I have heard about Jesus. A lot of people, mostly ordinary fishermen, have followed Him from the beginning, listening to His teaching. But now everyone has seen what He has done, so many people are following Jesus and learning from Him. The truly amazing thing is that this man is like a magician! He has fed thousands of people with just five loaves and two fish! He has healed lots of people – the blind, lepers, sick men and children, and even a woman and a servant! He casts out demons. He doesn't take money for any of this. They say He even raised people from the dead! How can a simple carpenter do things like that?

Jesus tells people that God loves them and that they should love each other. It's a pity the Romans don't think like that! I talked with my father about this.

"It is the feast of the Passover in just a few days, which celebrates how God freed His people from slavery in Egypt," my father said. "Jerusalem is full of visitors, Jews coming to celebrate the festival. They are all excited and longing for freedom from strict Roman rule. They might want Jesus to become their leader and fight for them against the Romans. The religious leaders are scared that Jesus will cause even more trouble, so they want to kill Him in secret, before that can happen."

That didn't sound right to me. I think Jesus sounds incredible, but my father works for Caiaphas, so he must do what the high priest tells him. But I wondered what my father *really* thinks about this man, Jesus.

There were lots of important priests and elders arriving at the house of Caiaphas to talk about what they were going to do. They were the important Jewish leaders in the city. My father is always telling me not to listen in to everything that happens in the high priest's house, but I still do it. These Jewish leaders really seemed to hate Jesus. It sounded as if they wanted to arrest Him!

Then another man arrived. Not dressed like the important leaders, he looked like a rough worker. I wondered what they wanted with him.

"My name is Judas," he said. "I am one

of Jesus' best friends. I can lead you to Him, if you pay me the money we agreed on, thirty pieces of silver."

"That's a lot of money," said one of the Jewish leaders. "I hear Jesus has lots of followers. He's always with them. How will we even know which one He is?"

"That's simple," said Judas eagerly. "They'll be in the place below the big orchard of olive trees. Jesus often goes there to pray. I know He's going there tonight because I've just had supper with them all. I'll go up to Jesus and kiss Him, as all men do when they meet. He'll think it's just another evening and that I've come to pray with them all. Then I'll leave quickly and the soldiers and the officers of the Temple guard can jump out and arrest Him."

I could see how anxious Judas was to get his hands on the leather bag of silver coins that the high priest had brought out.

What a rat! I thought.

They all talked quietly together for a moment, looking pleased with themselves. Then I had to move quickly as they all started coming into the courtyard where I'd been lurking. I got busy putting wood on the fire and tried to pretend I hadn't heard a word. One of them started barking orders.

"The soldiers and Temple guard are waiting outside. They are fully armed. Malchus, Caiaphas wants you to come with us and represent him. Judas, you go on ahead and we'll follow you."

I watched with despair as the group set out. Then the high priest turned back.

"You, boy!" he roared. "Yes, you! Light up a torch and walk ahead of them. It's getting dark already and they can hardly see a thing. Jump to it!"

With trembling hands I picked up a bundle of branches, full of resin, already tied together. Making torches was one of my jobs and I had to make sure there was always a good supply of them. I thrust the torch into the fire and it quickly caught on. Reluctantly I held it high above my head and walked ahead of the large group of men. I was glad when my father came to walk beside me.

We followed Judas through the still crowded streets. It was much quieter once we got outside the walls of the city. Then we reached the place. I knew it was where they press the olives to make the oil from the trees higher up the hill. Being at the head of the group, my father and I could see everything. The soldiers followed with their swords. The officers from the high priest and Temple guard lagged behind.

Between the trees there was a man kneeling down, obviously praying, and crying out to God. The group of men behind Him looked as if they might once have been praying. Now they were slumped and snoring. In the torchlight, the sweat on the man's face looked like drops of blood. He got up and went over to them.

"Are you going to sleep all night? My time is up, the Son of Man is about to be delivered into the hands of sinners. Get up! Let's get going! My betrayer is here."

Then Judas walked forward into the place and kissed this man on the cheek and said, "How are you, Teacher?" The man was Jesus.

The three men were now wide awake, looking amazed at the sight of Judas, followed by men armed with swords and clubs. They rushed to their leader's side, one of them drawing his sword.

"Are you betraying the Son of Man with a kiss?" said Jesus. "Stop pretending, Judas. Do what you came to do."

At that, the crowd of men behind me came forward and Judas ran away.

The men with Jesus came closer to defend Him.

"Shall we fight?" asked one.

But the other one didn't wait to ask for

permission. He rushed toward my father and sliced at his head with his sword. My father moved quickly, even though he hadn't expected the men to fight. Shocked, I dropped my torch on the ground. It still burned brightly, illuminating the horrible sight of my own father's *ear*. It lay on the ground beside him, and there was blood. It was *horrible*.

"No violence, Peter," said Jesus gently. "Put your sword back where it belongs. All who use swords will be destroyed by swords. Don't you realize that I am able right now to call to My Father, and twelve companies of fighting angels would be here to help Me? But I must do the job My Father has given Me, so I won't do that. If I did, how would the Scriptures come true, the ones that say this is the way it has to be?"

Then Jesus knelt to pick up my poor father's ear. He reached out and, for a moment, held it against my father's head.

When He stepped back, the ear was just as it had been before, firmly attached to his head. It was a miracle!

I expected everyone to gasp, to cry out that this was all a mistake! That this man, Jesus, really was a miracle worker! That He really must be the Son of God. But nobody did, not one of them! My father was still silent with shock, feeling his ear, and shaking his head in disbelief.

Then Jesus called out to the mob.

"What are you doing, coming after Me with swords and clubs as if I were a dangerous criminal? Day after day I have been sitting in the Temple teaching, and you never so much as lifted a hand against Me. You've done it this way to confirm what the Scriptures have said about My coming."

Then the soldiers and Temple guards rushed forward. They roughly grabbed Jesus and dragged Him away. I looked back to see all His followers running away in the opposite direction. As the mob hauled Jesus to the jail I wondered what would happen to Him.

Somehow it seemed that Jesus knew it would happen and was willing for it to happen. He believed that it was God's plan. As I walked home, holding tight to my father's bloodstained sleeve I truly believed that Jesus was the Son of God. Still clutching his healed ear, I was sure that my father now believed that too.

Jailbreak!

"Alex! Alexander! Where are you? You'll be late for school!"

It was my father's voice, crosser and even more impatient than usual. I hurried to his side. He's not a mean father, nothing like that, but he has a really difficult job and it makes him very short-tempered. He's in charge of the prison here in Philippi and works long hours with the nastiest of criminals. The police drag them into his jail at all hours of the day and night and my father has to sort them out.

Sometimes it sounds as if his bosses are just as bad. I'm not supposed to listen when he tells my mother about his problems, but his voice is so loud! It seems that the bosses hold my father responsible for any bad things the criminals do after they've been locked up in prison, which really doesn't seem fair. You'd think they couldn't get up to much, locked up in jail but you'd be surprised! But surely it's not my father's fault?

I rushed off to the Temple for my lessons. I'm doing well at those, so am rarely kept late to repeat my learning. I like this because it gives me a bit of free time to wander around and see what's going on before I have to get back to my chores at the jail.

I like to roam around the marketplace, to see all the bright and beautiful things on sale – the cloth, the foods, and the spices –

and to smell all the amazing smells. Most of all I like to watch the people. People come to Philippi from all over the place, all wearing different types of clothes and speaking different languages, or in strange accents. There's always something really interesting to watch.

I was just coming out into the sunlight when I noticed a commotion nearby. There's a noisy slave girl who always sits in the same place near the Temple. She's not selling anything though, she tells fortunes. The men who own her make a lot of money from the people who come and pay for her to tell their future. People want to know things like which field they should sow next, or who they should do business with. Anything they need to make a decision on really. Everyone knows she can see into the future and help them. That's why her owners are so rich.

I see her every day after my classes. For days she'd been following these two

strangers around and shouting at them.
I've heard they are called Paul and Silas.
They've been causing trouble here for
a while now. They tell stories about a
man called Jesus. They say that He was
dead but now He lives. They say that He
is the Son of the one true God Himself!
What nonsense! Here in Philippi, people
worship hundreds of gods. These
strangers from Judea tell a good story
though.

The local police don't like them
because there are always crowds of
people wanting to listen and they cause
obstruction in the marketplace. Today,
instead of ignoring her, as he usually did,
Paul stopped and turned to her.

"There is an evil demon in this poor
little girl!" he told the people. "I command
you, demon, in the name of Jesus Christ,
get out of her!"

The demon was gone, just like that.
Everyone could see how changed she

looked, no longer loud and confident. She looked just like any ordinary young girl.

"Get back to work!" ordered one of her owners. "Time is money and you're wasting it!"

The other turned to Paul and Silas and yelled at them menacingly.

"You strangers, leave! We don't want people like you around here, talking nonsense and holding up our business!"

But it soon became obvious that what Paul had done had not only held up their business, but ruined it forever. Without the evil demon, the slave girl just couldn't tell the future anymore.

As soon as they realized this, the two men roared with rage and went after Paul and Silas, beat them, dragged them into the market square, and called for the police.

Like many others, I followed, anxious to see what would happen.

"These men are disturbing the peace. They are dangerous troublemakers, trying to overthrow our way of life and challenge our laws!"

By this time the crowd had turned into an angry mob, all against the strangers.

I had to get back home then, so I didn't see what happened next, but I certainly heard about it afterwards. They soon went to court and were pronounced guilty. The judge ordered them to be beaten in the marketplace and sent to jail. When they were dragged to our prison, I was there with my father.

I've seen lots of criminals arriving at the prison. Some are angry, shouting and swearing, even as the police beat them and try to keep them quiet. Most are scared and cowering. These two men were different. They walked tall and dignified, as if they were on their way to the Temple, not about to be thrown into jail. They didn't shout and swear. They didn't even complain about the way they were being treated. Their clothes were torn and filthy from when the crowd had attacked them. They were bruised and bloodstained from their beating, but somehow they didn't look or act like any criminal I'd ever seen before.

"Lock up these dogs with your strongest chains!" the police said to my father. "Put them in the deepest, darkest dungeon! We don't want them escaping!"

I flinched when I saw Paul and Silas close up – their cuts and bruises looked so painful. My father and my older brother each grabbed one of the men and roughly herded them through the jail.

"Come along, Alex!" yelled my father. "Get the padlocks! We need you to help with the chains."

We passed all the strong stone cells with iron bars that were already filled with yelling, swearing prisoners. We went deep into the jail, where they'd dug out an inner room. I hated going in there. It was gloomy and scary – and always full of rats. I hate rats! There are always rats in a prison, but they usually run away when people approach. Here in this damp dark dungeon it seems as if the rats own the place.

My father and brother threw Paul and Silas onto the stone floor and quickly put leg irons on them, tethering them to the floor. There was no way they could escape those, but even more chains were wrapped around them. I handed out the padlocks, the heavy bag of them biting painfully into my shoulder. But I thought my pain must be nothing compared to what Paul and Silas felt.

As we left, Paul, and then Silas, started to sing. To sing in that dark, dirty, rat-infested jail cell! I turned around and gazed at them, my mouth open in shock. They sang as if they were happy – as if they were at a party or a festival.

"Alex! Stop gawping and get out of there!" my father ordered.

He and my older brother left the dungeon, taking the oil light and leaving

me in the dark with the prisoners – and
the rats. I tried to run after them but
immediately caught my foot in a loop of
chain and would have fallen, but for Paul's
hands, that caught me and gently put me
back on my feet, despite the weight of his
clanking chains.

I stumbled out after my father,
astounded and so confused. These were
supposed to be evil criminals, who had
come to harm Philippi. But they seemed
so calm – and kind! I didn't know what to
think.

I found it hard to get to sleep after that,
even if Paul and Silas hadn't been praying
and singing loudly all night. The other
prisoners couldn't believe their ears either,
but eventually I drifted off to sleep.

I woke as the ground beneath me began
to shake and wobble. It was as if a giant
had lifted my sleeping mat and tossed me
about like a leaf in the wind! It was a *huge*
earthquake!

I could hear people screaming and my father and my older brother cursing loudly. The whole jailhouse tottered and every door flew open.

"Quick!" roared Father. "We have to check the cells!"

Throwing on our tunics, we followed him toward the cells. It was as we feared, all the doors had opened and all the prisoners were free!

"I'm as good as dead," groaned my father, falling to his knees and drawing his sword. "I might as well kill myself now! The bosses will blame me for this and kill me slowly and painfully!"

"No!" we all yelled. My brother and I tried desperately to get to him and stop him. But it was the prisoner, Paul, who got there first.

"Don't do that! We're all still here!" said Paul. "Nobody's run away!"

Father got an oil lamp and ran to look. Paul was right. Paul and Silas must have been talking to the other prisoners all night, telling them stories about the man, Jesus, who was really the one true God. Everyone was still there, all eager to hear more.

My father collapsed in a heap in front of Paul and Silas.

Not only had the doors come off their hinges but the padlocks and the chains had all burst open. Surely an earthquake couldn't do all that!

"It must be true," he whispered. "Do you really serve the one true God? What do I have to do to be saved, to really live, as you do?"

"Put your trust in the Lord Jesus," said Paul. "If you and all your family put your entire trust in Him, then you'll live as you were meant to live on earth, then forever in heaven with Him!"

Father brought them over to our living quarters. Every one of us shared Mother's good food together as Paul and Silas spent the rest of the night telling us more about Jesus and what He did for us. Their wounds were bathed and bandaged. Mother mended their torn clothes. We had the best time ever! My whole family put our trust in God that night. Paul even baptized us so we all became part of the family of God.

The next day the court officials came to free Paul and Silas, as they hadn't realized that they were Roman citizens. Paul made them apologize to them too, for having them thrown in jail.

But I am so happy that it was my father's jail they were thrown into! Now my family and I can look forward to everlasting life with Jesus. What a celebration we had all enjoyed last night – for the jailbreak that never happened!